MONOPOLY

BY MARI BOLTE

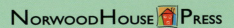

Norwood House Press

For information regarding Norwood House Press, please visit our website at www.norwoodhousepress.com or call 866-565-2900.

Credits
Editor: Kristy Stark
Designer: Sara Radka
Fact Checkers: Ann Schwab & Eleanor Cardell

Photo Credits
Getty Images: Alex Wong, 25, Cate Gillon, 30, Gareth Cattermole, 33, Ian Waldie, 42, Lisa Maree Williams, 13, martince2, cover, 1, 19, 20, 21, Matt Winkelmeyer, 26, mattjeacock, 3, 10, Picture Post, 6, Radu Bercan, 7; Newscom: Hasbro/Splash, 9, Imaginechina/Splash News, 29; Shutterstock: Alex_Po, 36, Anneke Swanepoel, 34, Ben Molyneux, 5, Casimiro PT, 37, DerekTeo, 23, digitalreflections, 39, EWY Media, 40, John Gome, 22, Par To Perfect, 11, PhotographerIncognito, 41, Rosemarie Mosteller, 17, S Usharani, 4, 35, TonelsonProductions, 15, txking, 16

Library of Congress Cataloging-in-Publication Data
Names: Bolte, Mari, author.
Title: Monopoly / by Mari Bolte.
Description: Chicago : Norwood House Press, 2022. | Series: A great game! |
    Includes index. | Audience: Ages 8-10 | Audience: Grades 4-6 |
    Summary: "An introductory look at the board game Monopoly. Describes the history of the game, introduces the creators and innovators, highlights competitions, and provides insight about the game's future. Informational text for readers who are new to Monopoly, or are interested in learning more. Includes a glossary, index, and bibliography for further reading. Explores the board game Monopoly, from its early origins as a statement against tycoons and their business monopolies, to the popular family-friendly game we know today"--Provided by publisher.
Identifiers: LCCN 2021049727 (print) | LCCN 2021049728 (ebook) | ISBN 9781684507931
    (hardcover) | ISBN 9781684047253 (paperback) | ISBN 9781684047291 (epub)
Subjects: LCSH: Monopoly (Game)--Juvenile literature.
Classification: LCC GV1469.M65 B64 2022 (print) | LCC GV1469.M65 (ebook) | DDC 794--dc23/eng/20211109
LC record available at https://lccn.loc.gov/2021049727
LC ebook record available at https://lccn.loc.gov/2021049728

Hardcover ISBN: 978-1-68450-793-1
Paperback ISBN: 978-1-68404-725-3

Monopoly™ is a registered trademark of HASBRO, INC.
This book is not associated with Monopoly™, HASBRO, INC., or any of its associated partners.

©2022 by Norwood House Press. All rights reserved.
No part of this book may be reproduced without written permission from the publisher.
347N—012022
Manufactured in the United States of America in North Mankato, Minnesota.

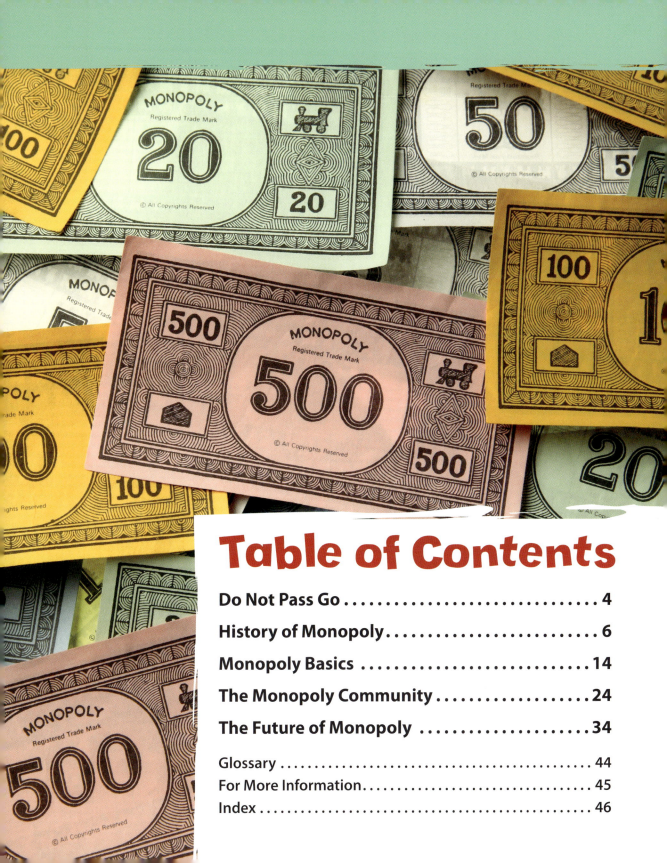

Table of Contents

Do Not Pass Go 4
History of Monopoly 6
Monopoly Basics 14
The Monopoly Community 24
The Future of Monopoly 34

Glossary 44
For More Information 45
Index 46

Do Not Pass Go

It's your turn. You hold two dice in your hand. You need to move eight spaces to land on the property you need.

You hold your breath and roll the dice. Double fours! You move your token ahead to the property. You pay for it. You have your first **Monopoly**!

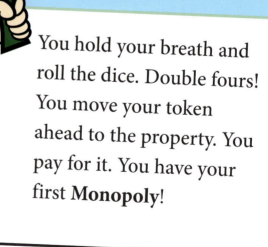

Monopoly can be played by two to eight players.

Doubles mean you get to take another turn. Two twos move you to Chance. The card tells you to take $25. Will your luck continue? One last roll. Doubles again! Three doubles in a row send you to Jail. You do not pass Go. You do not collect $200. This is the world of Monopoly.

History of Monopoly

In 1904, Lizzie G. Magie created the first version of what we know today as Monopoly. Her game was called The Landlord's Game. Players circled a game board collecting money, paying rent, and buying railroads. There was fake money for borrowing and spending. **Deeds** and properties could be bought and sold. Players had to pay taxes. The game also had the famous "Go to Jail" corner on the board.

There were two ways to play. In one, everyone was rewarded when there was money. In the other, the goal was to crush the other players. The Landlord's Game was meant to show how hoarding huge amounts of money hurt everyone else.

DID YOU KNOW?

Board games were popular during the Great Depression (1929–1939). People did not have money to go out or buy new things. But board games were inexpensive and could be played many times. Scrabble and Sorry! are other Depression-era games.

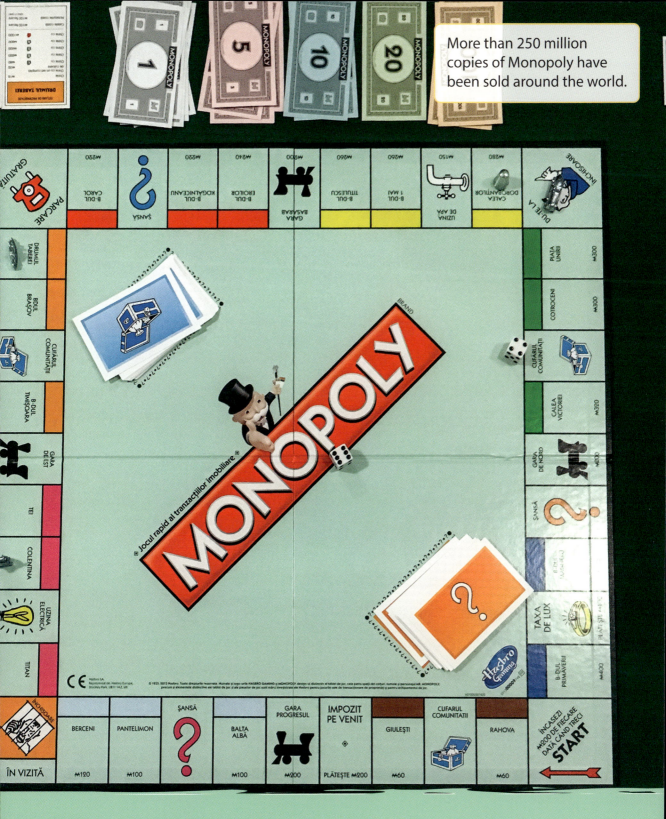

More than 250 million copies of Monopoly have been sold around the world.

Magie **patented** her board game. When she renewed the patent in 1924, less than one percent of all patents were filed by women. And the patent protected her idea. Other inventors could not get patents for games like hers. Their games were too similar.

But patents did not stop people from copying popular games or ideas. The Landlord's Game was one of those. Around 1933, Charles B. Darrow started selling his own version. But he couldn't make it fast enough. So, he sold it to Parker Brothers. They loved the idea. They sold Monopoly as a game invented by an out-of-work engineer just looking for fun.

Parker Brothers bought Magie's patent from her in 1935. Magie was hoping they would want her to do more work for them. They didn't. But Darrow became a millionaire.

Who Was Lizzie G. Magie?

Lizzie G. Magie was born in 1866. She was unusual for her time. She did not marry until she was 44 years old. She had a job, wrote poetry, and was a stage actress and comedian.

Magie never got over Darrow stealing her idea. She had made $500 from Monopoly from her patents. It probably cost her more money to develop and produce the game than she ever made from it. She went uncredited until 1973, when a researcher uncovered the truth.

Charles Darrow sold his version of Monopoly for $4 per game. He would be a millionaire just a year after selling the rights to Parker Brothers.

History of Monopoly: Time Line

1904
Lizzie G. Magie patents the first version of Monopoly. She calls it The Landlord's Game.

1924
Magie renews her patent on The Landlord's Game.

1933
Charles B. Darrow starts selling his own version of Magie's game. Later, he sells the game to Parker Brothers. Parker Brothers buys Magie's copyright two years later.

1983
Parker Brothers loses the trademark to the name Monopoly.

1991
Hasbro buys the toy company Tonka, which includes the rights to Parker Brothers and all the company's board games.

By 1935, Parker Brothers was ready to sell Monopoly. There were two editions: Standard and Deluxe. Standard cost $2. It sold 278,000 copies in its first year. The next year, sales topped 1,750,000 copies. The company made more than $2 million in profit. That's more than $39 million today! For the next 30 years, Monopoly would sell around one million copies a year.

In the 1930s, Parker Brothers **sued** Milton Bradley. Their game, Easy Money, was very similar.

Real Monopolies

Monopolies are large companies or corporations that control the entire industry. This allows them to control the price of the goods and services they offer. For example, if only one company offered cell phone service, you would have to use them or go without a cell phone. They could charge whatever price they wanted. There would be no competition. Facebook and Microsoft are examples of monopolies.

In 1973, Ralph Anspach released a game called Anti-Monopoly. Players take on the role of lawyers. Their job is to break up price-gouging monopolies. It sold 200,000 copies. But it also caught the attention of Parker Brothers. In 1974, they sued Anspach.

Anspach won his court case in 1983. Parker Brothers lost the **trademark** to the name Monopoly. The court said that the name generically described the product, not the specific game. When a name becomes commonly used, the trademark is lost. Other examples of this include escalator, thermos, and trampoline. Anspach's game about breaking up monopolies had broken up the Monopoly monopoly.

In 1991, Hasbro bought the Tonka toy company. This included Parker Brothers and all the games they published. Today, Hasbro is one of the largest toy and game companies in the world. They have owned around 85 percent of all board games since the late 1990s. They started making different versions of Monopoly. This made the game even more popular. Today, Monopoly sales account for one-third of all board games sold around the world.

DID YOU KNOW?
J. P. Morgan had a monopoly in railroads. He is said to be the inspiration for Rich Uncle Pennybags, also known as Mr. Monopoly.

Losing the trademark hasn't slowed down fans of the game. Monopoly is sold in more than 110 countries and in 47 different languages.

Monopoly Basics

Monopoly is a game for two to eight players. There is a board, two dice, game pieces or tokens, 32 houses, and 12 hotels. Each property has a Title Deed. The object of the game is to buy, rent, and sell property to become the richest player.

The game starts with one player being the Banker/**Auctioneer**. The Bank holds the Title Deeds, cards, houses and hotels, and the money. The Banker hands out money to each player at the beginning of the game. Everyone gets $1,500. The rest of the money stays in the Bank. The Bank never goes broke.

DID YOU KNOW?

The squares that have the highest chance of a player ending up on them are Jail, Illinois Avenue, and Go. The orange properties and the railroads are also high-probability spaces. The chances of landing on the Chance and Community Chest squares are lower. No properties send players to them, so they must be landed on by rolls only.

There are 28 Title Deed cards in each game.

Every time Go is passed, the player gets $200.

Every player starts on Go. They take turns by rolling the dice. The numbers on the dice determine how far they move. The game board has 40 spaces. There are 10 squares along every edge. Each square represents railroads, utilities, Jail, or 28 properties.

The space the player lands on determines their action. If the player lands on a property owned by another player, they must pay rent to the owner. If the property is unowned, they can buy it. If they do not want the property, it is auctioned off. Anyone can bid. The winner receives the Deed Title, which is placed face-up in front of the player. The Deed Titles indicate the **mortgage** value of the property, as well as rent values.

Players can mortgage Deed Titles for money. The mortgage gets the owner half of the property's value in money. Once mortgaged, the Deed Title card must be flipped over. No rent can be collected on mortgaged properties. To pay off the mortgage, the owner must pay the amount of the mortgage plus 10 percent. If the mortgage is paid off, the card can be placed face-up again.

DID YOU KNOW?

The Monopoly property Marvin Gardens is named after a neighborhood in Atlantic City, New Jersey. The actual neighborhood is called Marven Gardens, but it was misspelled on the game.

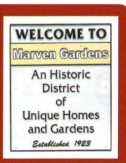

The properties on the game board are organized by color. When a player owns all the properties in one color group, that is a monopoly. This doubles the properties' rent. The property owner can also buy houses and hotels, which can add hundreds of dollars to the rent.

The maximum number of houses on a single property is four. Then they can be returned to the bank and exchanged for a hotel. Only one hotel can be built on each property. Unimproved properties can be sold, but not the buildings. Buildings must be sold back to the bank—at half price—before the property can be exchanged.

Monopoly Tips

Check out these tips from the 2015 UK and Ireland Monopoly champion, Natalie Fitzsimons, on how to win.

- Borrow as much as you can and spend it on upgrading monopolies.
- Buying three houses gives the biggest return. But buying as many as possible means someone else goes without.
- Go to Jail. Stay there as long as you can.
- Never buy Park Place. It is expensive and rarely landed on.
- Form alliances with other players. Team up to collect and trade properties. Sell them to allies for low prices.

Boardwalk is the most expensive property. It also has the highest rent.

In 2008, the Chance and Community Chest cards were standardized. This means that the cards are the same no matter what country you are in. The only differences are the names of the properties.

Some squares are not properties. Players who land on Chance or Community Chest must draw a card. The cards direct the players on what to do next. They might have to move to another square. They might award the player small cash prizes. Some cards send players to Jail. Other cards get them out of Jail for free.

When a player goes to Jail, they cannot collect their $200 for passing Go. They can get out of Jail by using a "Get Out of Jail Free" card. They can also roll doubles on any of their next three turns or pay a $50 fine.

Players travel around the board until they go **bankrupt**. The last player that is not bankrupt is the winner.

DID YOU KNOW?

Free Parking is just a blank space on the board. Some people play by putting fees or jail fines aside and awarding them to whoever lands on Free Parking. However, this is not an official Monopoly rule.

Each player selects a token at the beginning of the game. The token is what moves around the game board. The original tokens were the thimble, top hat, shoe, cannon, battleship, and iron. The top hat is based on the one Mr. Monopoly wears.

Pieces added later include the rocking horse, race car, Scottie dog, wheelbarrow, horse and rider, and cat. Some pieces have been retired. They were replaced by newer shapes. In 2017, people got to vote online for new pieces. There were 64 choices. Emojis, a cell phone, a roller skate, and a hashtag were some of the options. T-rex, rubber ducky, and penguin were the most popular.

The original game had six tokens. Today, there are eight tokens because the game is for two to eight players. Some versions of Monopoly have up to 12 tokens.

DID YOU KNOW?

The biggest Monopoly token in the world is of the car token. It is nine feet, eight inches (2.96 meters) long, three feet, one inch (0.955 m) wide, and four feet, two inches (1.285 m) tall. The car is on display at Monopoly Dreams in Hong Kong.

The pieces in your Monopoly set can tell you how old your game actually is.

The Monopoly Community

Monopoly is the fourth best-selling board game of all time. It is behind only chess, checkers, and backgammon. All three of those games date back thousands of years. Over 200 million copies of Monopoly have been sold since Parker Brothers put out the first version in 1935. More than one billion people have passed Go.

Monopoly has been played on a ceiling, underground, underwater, and in a nuclear submarine. The longest game ever played lasted 70 days. The longest game in a bathtub lasted 99 hours. And the longest upside-down game went on for a day and a half!

Tournament of Champions

Official Monopoly tournaments have their own rules. Players cannot bring anything with them when they sit down at the board. There are time limits to keep games moving. At the end of the time limit, the players' **assets** are totaled. Assets include cash, property ownership, houses, and hotels. The top two or four players move on to the next round. The final round might go on until only one player is left.

The 2009 U.S. National Monopoly Championship was played at Union Station in Washington, D.C.

25

Daymond John is a businessman, investor, writer, and speaker. He founded the clothing brand FUBU and has been on the TV show *Shark Tank*.

On May 20, 2021, Hasbro hosted the Monopoly Charity Classic. It was aired on YouTube. The celebs were playing for a $350,000 Community Chest fund for the charities of their choice. Ellie Kemper, Josh Gad, Tiffany Haddish, and Daymond John were the competitors.

The game had special rules. It started by giving the players randomly selected properties. The youngest player went first. Landing on a Community Chest space meant that players had to exit Jail on their next turn.

The game lasted an hour. Daymond John came out on top, winning extra cash for My Brother's Keeper Alliance. The organization works to build safe and supportive communities for boys and young men of color.

Ticket to Freedom

During World War II (1939–1945), British prisoners of war received copies of Monopoly. The games were part of a care package to help them get through their imprisonment. But when they looked inside, they found compasses and metal files among the game pieces. There was real money. A map was hidden on the specially marked game board. The game boxes were the perfect size to hide everything a soldier needed to escape from behind enemy lines. Thousands of POWs used Monopoly to free themselves.

The first Monopoly World Championship was held in 1973. Since then, there have been 13 more championships.

The 2015 World Championship was held in Macao, China. Twenty-eight players won spots in the championship game by becoming the top player in their own countries. Italian player Nicolò Falcone won the prize of $20,580, the amount of money in the "bank."

The 2021 Championship was supposed to be held in Hong Kong but was canceled because of the COVID-19 pandemic.

Under the Boardwalk

In 2011, a documentary about the World Championships came out. *Under The Boardwalk: The Monopoly Story* told the stories of the people who competed for the title. The filmmakers followed them to the championship held that year in Las Vegas. They explored the psychology behind the game and the best strategies to come out on top. They also talked about the history of the game. *Under the Boardwalk's* website posts photos and updates about the championships for any interested fans.

Monopoly champion Nicolò Falcone took the top prize the same year Monopoly turned 80.

British Monopoly players get £200 instead of $200 when they pass Go.

Older, retired tokens include the iron, thimble, horse, boot, cannon, purse, and lantern. Finding out when the piece was part of the game can help pinpoint the age of the Monopoly set. For instance, the Scottie dog was not added until the 1950s. The rocking horse was only part of the game between the 1930s and 1950s.

The United States' version of the game uses real street names from Atlantic City, New Jersey. But Monopoly can be found in more than 45 countries. The games usually use locations from the country in which it is sold. For example, England's version uses London street names. Baltic and Mediterranean Avenue are changed to Whitechapel and Old Kent Roads.

Twice-Used Tokens

During World War II, the demand for metal was high. Tokens were made of wood, compressed paper and sawdust, cardboard, or Bakelight, an early type of plastic.

Most Monopoly pieces today are made of pewter. But in 1991, Parker Brothers released the Franklin Mint version of Monopoly. The houses were coated in silver, and the pieces and hotels were coated in gold. The Chance and Community Chest cards had gold foil decorations.

There are all sorts of official ways to play Monopoly. The Cheater's Version tells players to break the rules to win. But players caught cheating are handcuffed to the Jail space.

Monopoly for Millennials encourages players to gain experiences, rather than money. They travel around the game board finding new places to eat, shop, and hang out with friends.

Monopoly for Sore Losers issued a challenge: Don't get sad. Get even! Useless tasks, like a player landing on their own property, earn Sore Loser coins. Sore loser coins can also be stolen. Enough coins buy the Mr. Monopoly token. The token gives the ability to stomp around the board and take money.

Longest Game Ever adds extra properties. It also has only one die. The game does not end until a single player owns every property on the board. But Monopoly Speed exists too. It can be played in 10 minutes or less! There are only four rounds. Players race against a timer to buy, sell, and trade properties.

DID YOU KNOW?

Monopoly fans have had a say in how their favorite game grows and changes. In early 2021, they could vote on new Community Chest cards. "Shop Local", "Rescue a Puppy", and "Help Your Neighbors" were ideas. The updated cards were included in the fall 2021 game release.

Monopoly Revolution was a version that didn't use paper money. Instead, an electronic reader kept track of players' income through debit card swipes.

The Future of Monopoly

Monopoly adapted to the twenty-first century when UbiSoft made it into a video game in 2017. Monopoly Plus can be played with a flat game board. But it also has a live game board with a full 3-D city. The rules can be changed. Games can be saved and picked up later. Groups can play together in person. A single player can also join an online game with strangers.

Monopoly is also on the App Store and Google Play. It can also be played across platforms. So, friends can play together online from their Apple and Android devices. People even play together on Zoom or Skype!

DID YOU KNOW?
In the past, Monopoly has been banned in some countries. Places like the former Soviet Union, China, and Cuba thought it was too focused on **capitalism**.

Each neighborhood in Monopoly Plus is animated with its own personality, including tiny shops, cars, and people.

Some estimate that more than 1,100 versions of Monopoly exist around the world.

Hasbro has stopped thinking up new games. Instead, they have been making new versions of existing games. Between 1995 and 2005, around 230 official versions of Monopoly were created. Today, there are hundreds of **licensed** versions. There are also expansion packs, travel-size sets, dice games, and other Monopoly-related items.

Expansion packs and special editions have kept the game fresh. Stock Exchange was one of the first. It lets players buy and sell stock. It originally came out in 1936. Today, players can download the certificates and rules for free.

Personalizing Monopoly boards dates way back to Lizzie G. Magie's version. People changed the property names to local places. Today, custom Monopoly boards are given as gifts and sold to fundraise. People can even make their own online game with My Monopoly. The games can be played on consoles or computers. Photos can be uploaded and printed as stickers. The stickers are for customized tokens and cards.

DID YOU KNOW?

Hasbro's website has 240 games that can be played online. Forty-five of those games are different kinds of Monopoly.

Customized Monopoly boards are still the original game, just with different locations. But there are also other ways to play the game. Monopoly Deal and Monopoly Bid are card games. In Deal, players must collect properties, like in the original game. Up to five players can play the game in as little as fifteen minutes. Bid is a game of chance. Players participate in auctions to collect property cards.

Monopoly Junior came out in 1990. It has fewer pieces, a smaller board, and kid-friendly locations.

Don't Go to Jail and Monopoly Express are dice games. Players earn points, money, or properties by rolling the dice.

McDonald's Monopoly

The first McDonald's Monopoly started in 1987. Certain food items came with random stickers that looked like Monopoly cards. The cards could be collected and traded in for prizes. Prizes ranged from free fries to piles of cash. People around the world look forward to peeling stickers off fries, chicken nuggets, or drink cups to see if they've won the grand prize, which is usually $1 million. In 2016 alone, 500 million stickers were printed. Some people couldn't wait for their next value meal, though. One man figured out a way to cheat. Over several years, he stole more than $24 million in cash and prizes before being caught.

Monopoly Deal comes with 110 cards. They represent properties, rent, houses and hotels, and money.

Monopoly in the Park is located in San Jose, California. It is the largest permanent Monopoly board in the world.

Fans of Monopoly can show off with officially branded shoes, t-shirts, bags, and more. There are even Funko POP! figures of Mr. Monopoly.

Unofficial items are out there too. Pillows and blankets, wall art, ornaments, and face masks are only a few things fans have made. Other people sell things to make playing the game easier. Cash and card holders, wooden boards, 3-D printed houses, and custom money and tokens can add to the game experience.

There are even tiny and huge versions! The world's smallest game fits inside a three-inch (1.2-cm) carrying case. It comes with dice, tokens, houses and hotels, cards, money, and the board. The world's largest is 9,690 square feet (900.228 square meters).

DID YOU KNOW?

In 2008, it was announced that Ridley Scott would direct a movie based on Monopoly. It was going to be a comedy, with a good guy defeating the evil Parker Brothers. But so far, the movie hasn't moved much past an idea.

People could play a huge version of Monopoly in Sydney, Australia, in 2005. The board was 4,736 square feet (440 square meters) large.

Playing Monopoly in real life has gone beyond a paper board and some tiny tokens. A theme park called Monopoly Dream in Hong Kong, China, opened in 2019. Players enter Mr. Monopoly's secret residence. They can also visit the Bank, Water Works, Electric Company, and more. A mysterious man is hiding in Mr. Monopoly's home. He plans to steal something valuable. Visitors work to stop his plan.

A similar park opened in London in August 2021. Monopoly Lifesized is owned by Hasbro. It is a 4-D escape room experience. Players move around the 50-by-50-foot (15-by-15-meter) board. The game takes about 80 minutes to play and is part Monopoly game, part murder mystery. Players take on challenges to collect properties. Between eight and 24 people can play in four teams. There are also four different boards to choose from: Classic, Vault, City, and Junior.

Whether fans are playing the classic version or a new twist, Monopoly has shown that it has real star power!

DID YOU KNOW?
Monopoly was **inducted** into the National Toy Hall of Fame in 1998.

Glossary

assets: resources owned by a person or company that have financial value

auctioneer: a person who runs a public sale where people bid on goods and property

bankrupt: a person or business unable to repay outstanding debts

capitalism: an economic system where trade and businesses are controlled by private owners for profit

deeds: documents proving ownership of a property or asset

inducted: admission of someone or something into an organization

licensed: having permission to use another brand or intellectual property

monopoly: having complete control over the supply of a service or resource

mortgage: using property to get a loan for money

patented: an obtained license that gives an inventor exclusive ownership to an invention

sued: to bring legal action against someone or something

trademark: a symbol or word legally registered to a company or product

For More Information

Books

Polinsky, Paige V. *Monopoly Mastermind: Charles B. Darrow.* Minneapolis: Checkerboard Library, an imprint of Abdo Publishing, 2018.

Stone, Tanya Lee. *Pass Go and Collect $200: The Real Story of How Monopoly Was Invented.* New York: Henry Holt and Company, 2018.

Websites

Monopoly Patent (https://www.loc.gov/rr/business/businesshistory/December/monopoly.html) Learn about Monopoly's patent from the Library of Congress.

National Toy Hall of Fame (https://www.toyhalloffame.org/toys/monopoly) Monopoly's official page on the National Toy Hall of Fame website.

Index

Anspach, Ralph, 12

Anti-Monopoly, 12

Atlantic City, New Jersey, 17, 31

China, 28, 34, 43

Cuba, 34

Darrow, Charles B., 8, 10

Facebook, 11

Falcone, Nicolò, 28

Fitzsimons, Natalie, 18

Great Depression, 6

Hasbro, 10, 12, 27, 37, 43

John, Daymond, 27

Landlord's Game, The, 6, 8, 10

Magie, Lizzie G., 6, 8, 10, 37

McDonald's, 38

Microsoft, 11

monopolies, 11, 12, 18

Monopoly Charity Classic, 27

Morgan, J.P., 12

Mr. Monopoly, 12, 22, 32, 41, 43

online, 22, 34, 37

Parker Brothers, 8, 10, 11, 12, 24, 31, 41

Scrabble, 6

Sorry!, 6

Soviet Union, 34

tournaments, 24

versions, 12, 22, 37, 41

World War II, 27, 31

About the Author

Mari Bolte has worked in publishing as a writer and editor for more than 15 years. She has written dozens of books about things like science and craft projects, historical figures and events, and pop culture. She lives in Minnesota.